Please Don't Swat!

First paperback edition June 2022

ISBN: 979-8-9861997-1-9

Also available in hardcover and as a color Kindle ebook

Author website: kturnerauthor.com

Hello, it's so nice to meet you.

My name is Emmylou.

Wait, please don't run away in fright.

I promise you that I won't bite.

I'm not scary. I'm just a little honey bee as you can see.

And it's very, very cool

to be a bee like me.

I'm yellow and brown, and
I love flying through the air.

So do all my friends. Can you
see them over there?

I'm an insect. And in spite of my small size...

Insect – A small animal whose body is divided into three parts. Insects also have three pairs of legs, and usually one or two pairs of wings.

I have **2** antennaes,

6 legs,

and **5** eyes!

With all of those eyes on my head...

I can see every color except

RED!

To attract more bees to your garden, plant flowers that are violet, purple, and blue.

While bees cannot see red very well, they can detect ultra violet markings in red flowers.

My home is way up, up, up in a tree.

It's the perfect spot for a
bee like me.

The nest I live in

is called a hive.

And it's so much

FUN

to come flying out

of there

in a big high dive!

Inside the hive is my colony. There are worker bees, drones, and a

QUEEN.

Colony – An organized community of people, or insects, living and working together in the same place.

You should see it.

It's quite a scene.

Worker bees – Worker bees forage for food, build and protect the hive, clean, and circulate air by beating their wings. Worker bees are all female.

Drones – Drones are male honey bees, and they have just one job; to mate with the Queen in order to produce baby bees.

Queen – The queen honey bee plays a vital role in the hive. She produces a chemical scent that helps to regulate the unity of the colony, and lay eggs.

Did you know male honey bees don't have stingers? Only us girls do!

But there's no need to worry.

We're not interested in you.

Stinger – The sharp, pointed part of certain animals and plants that sometimes carry poisons.

I spend my day collecting pollen from flowers.

Bees use their straw like mouth to suck nectar from flowers and collect it in a little sac called a crop. They also collect pollen on their legs.

I can do this for hours and hours.

A bee will visit 50 to 100 flowers during each pollen collection trip.

It takes one bee 8 hours a day for 30 days to gather 1 teaspoon dose of pollen.

I may sound noisy, but it's because my wings are always beating.

Honey bees can beat their wings over 230 times per second.

Round and round the flowers
as the nectar I am eating.

Nectar – The sweet liquid which a plant makes that attracts birds and insects.

Bees need 3 things to survive: food, water, and shelter. They eat nectar, pollen, and honey.

Some of the pollen I collect falls onto other plants which helps them grow.

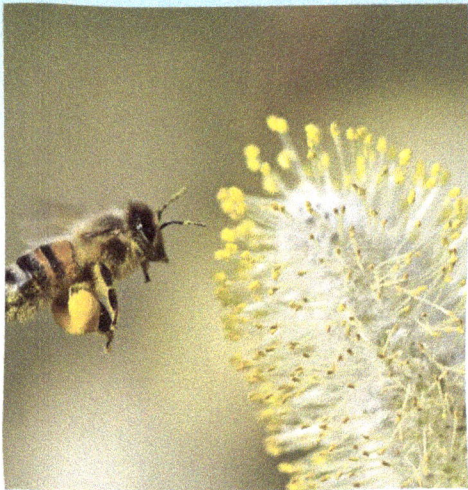

Pollinate – To move or carry pollen to a plant, causing the seeds to be fertilized.

So, be sure to thank a bee like me when your fruits and vegetables are sprouting up in a row.

I then take the rest of the pollen back to my nest.

And that's where I do what
honey bees do best.

We make honey that's yummy and sweet.

It's just the thing when you're in the mood for a tasty treat.

Honey

Honey bees are important to caring for our planet. So please help us take care by showing great thought.

Bees play a role in every aspect of our ecosystem. As pollinators, they support the growth of trees, flowers, and plants which then serve as food and shelter for both humans and other creatures.

You can do this by learning more about bees, telling your friends, and whatever you do...

Please
don't swat!

Glossary

Insect
A small animal whose body is divided into three parts. Insects also have three pairs of legs and usually one or two pairs of wings.

Antennae
A pair of long, thin body parts located on the head, which are used to feel and smell.

Stinger
The sharp, pointed part of certain animals and plants that sometimes carry poisons.

Worker bees
Worker bees forage for food, build and protect the hive, clean, and circulate air by beating their wings. Worker bees are all female.

Drones
Drones are male honey bees, and they have just one job: to mate with the queen in order to produce baby bees.

Queen
The queen honey bee plays a vital role in the hive. She produces a chemical scent that helps to regulate the unity of the colony, and lays eggs.

Nectar
The sweet liquid which a plant makes that attracts birds and insects.

Colony
An organized community of people, or insects, living and working together in the same place. Honey bee colonies consist of worker bees, drones, and a queen.

Hive
Something built for, or by, bees to live in.

Pollinate
To move or carry pollen to a plant, causing the seeds to be fertilized.

Honey
A thick, sweet liquid made from flower nectar by bees.

Beekeeper
A person who owns and cares for bees; they also collect their honey.

Life Cycle of a Honey Bee

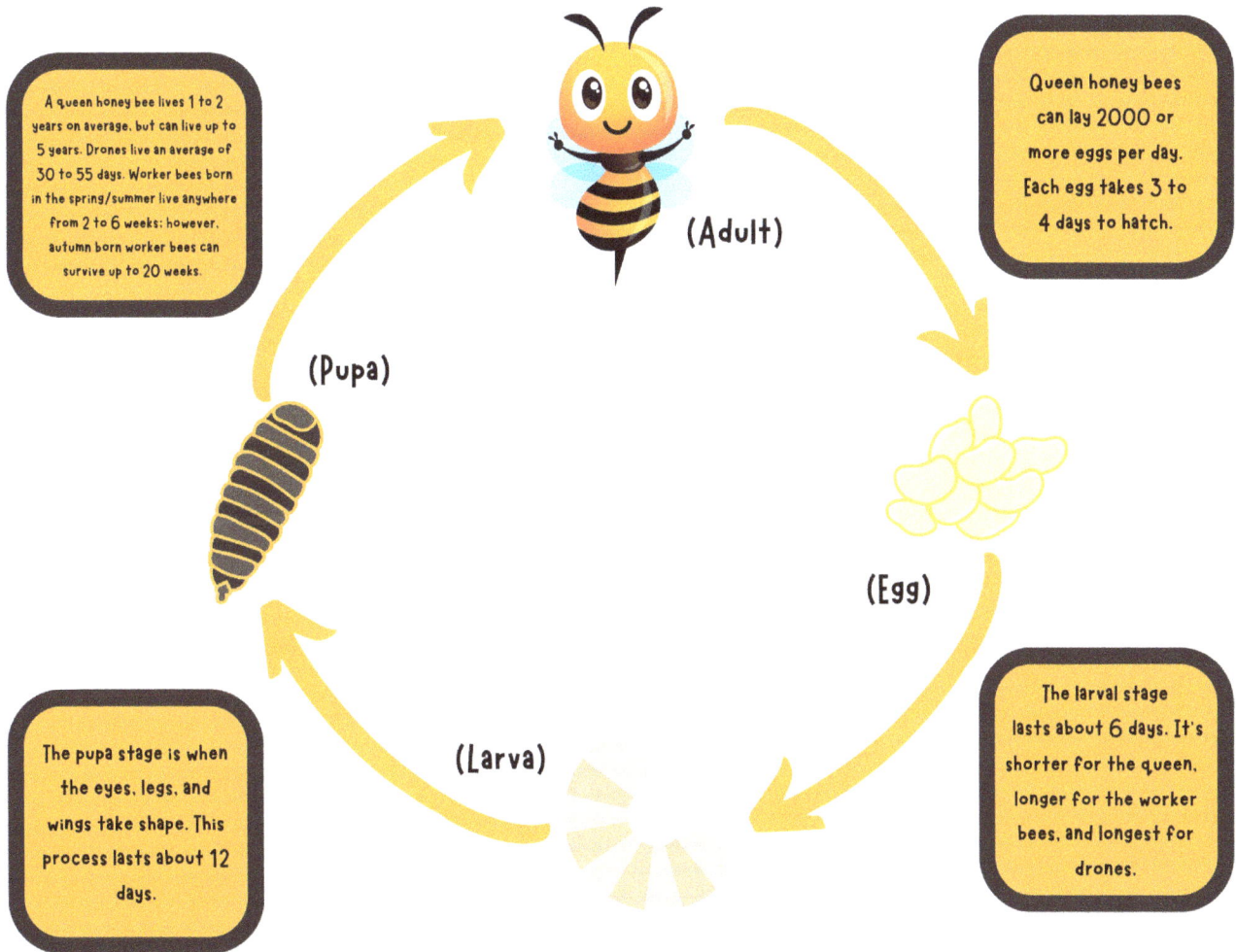

A queen honey bee lives 1 to 2 years on average, but can live up to 5 years. Drones live an average of 30 to 55 days. Worker bees born in the spring/summer live anywhere from 2 to 6 weeks; however, autumn born worker bees can survive up to 20 weeks.

(Adult)

Queen honey bees can lay 2000 or more eggs per day. Each egg takes 3 to 4 days to hatch.

(Pupa)

(Egg)

The pupa stage is when the eyes, legs, and wings take shape. This process lasts about 12 days.

(Larva)

The larval stage lasts about 6 days. It's shorter for the queen, longer for the worker bees, and longest for drones.

Bee Activities for Children

1. Plan a field trip to visit with a local beekeeper.

2. Get outside and go on a bee hunt. Make a game out of it by counting how many you see and how many flowers they land on. *But remember, observe and don't disturb.

3. Plant a garden with some bee friendly plants and flowers.

4. Visit your local library to do research and learn more about honey bees.

*(Some activities may not be appropriate for children who are allergic to bees.)

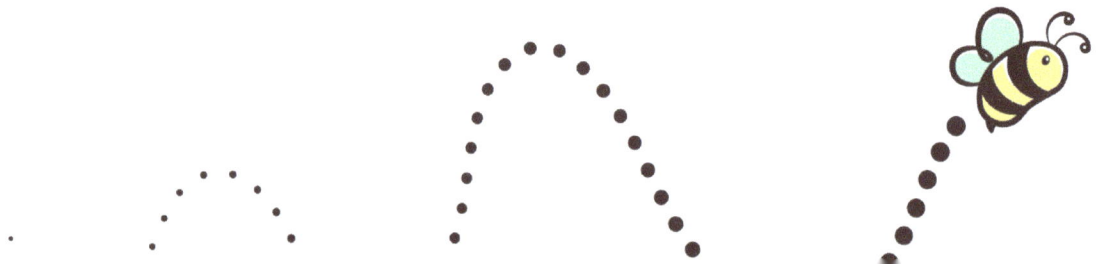

Discover more titles by the same author
@ kturnerauthor.com

Including these, and more!